FREDDIE PRINZE, JR.

A Real-Life Reader Biography

Wayne Wilson

Mitchell Lane Publishers, Inc.
P.O. Box 619 • Bear, Delaware 19701

Second Printing

Real-Life Reader Biographies

Library of Congress Cataloging-in-Publication Data
Wilson, Wayne, 1953-
     Freddie Prinze, Jr./Wayne Wilson.
        p. cm. — (A real-life reader biography)
     Includes index.
     ISBN 1-58415-063-7
     1. Prinze, Freddie, Jr.—Juvenile literature. 2. Motion picture actors and actresses—United States—Biography—Juvenile literature. [1. Prinze, Freddie, Jr. 2. Actors and actresses. 3. Hispanic Americans—Biography.] I. Title. II. Series.
PN2287.P714 W55 2000
791.43'028'092—dc21
[B]
                                                     00-034924

ABOUT THE AUTHOR: Wayne Wilson was born and raised in Los Angeles. He received a Master of Arts in Education from the University of California, Los Angeles. For 16 years he was co-owner and president of a pioneering and innovative publishing company specializing in multicultural designs. Recently he completed interviews with influential Latino men throughout the country and wrote over 160 biographies for *Encuentros: Hombre A Hombre*, a comprehensive vocational education book to be published by the California Department of Education. Several of Wilson's short stories have been published in commercial and literary magazines. Wilson lives in Venice Beach, California with his wife and daughter and is currently working on his first novel and screenplay.

PHOTO CREDITS: Cover: Globe Photos; p. 4 Corbis/Mitch Gerber; p. 7 The Kobal Collection; p. 8 Frank Edwards/Fotos International/Archive Photos; p. 18 Globe Photos; p. 19 The Kobal Collection; p. 21, 22 Globe Photos; p. 25 Lisa Rose/Globe Photos; p. 28 Corbis

ACKNOWLEDGMENTS: The following story has been thoroughly researched, and to the best of our knowledge, represents a true story. While every possible effort has been made to ensure accuracy, the publisher will not assume liability for damages caused by inaccuracies in the data, and makes no warranty on the accuracy of the information contained herein. This story has not been authorized by Freddie Prinze, Jr. or any of his representatives.

Table of Contents

Chapter 1
A World of Make-Believe

In high school, Freddie Prinze, Jr., was relentlessly teased and called a weirdo. On *The Tonight Show with Jay Leno* he said that his therapist told him, "All you do is live in other people's lives... you're never going to exist in the real world." Even he admits to being a little strange, and recalls spending much of his time in a fantasy world, pretending to be comic book heroes like the X-Men. Some of his classmates remember seeing him battling imaginary villains on the playing field after school.

Freddie Prinze, Jr. recalls spending much of his time in a fantasy world.

"My whole life I've always been on the outside looking in; I've never fit in, and I love it like that," Freddie told *The Los Angeles Times*. Fortunately, he has been able to parlay his talents for playing make-believe characters onto the big-screen. Freddie, the star of *I Know What You Did Last Summer* and *She's All That*, has shown refreshing vulnerability and down-to-earth charms that have led to his rapidly increasing popularity. The *Times* anointed the handsome six-foot-one brown-eyed actor "America's newest male star with superstar potential."

Although his mother is now one of his biggest supporters, initially she wanted her son to be anything but an actor. And no one could blame her when she strongly objected to his leaving Albuquerque, New Mexico, to pursue an acting career in Los Angeles, California. Her greatest fear was that Freddie would tread down the same path as his father.

Born on March 8, 1976, Freddie was only ten months old when his father, Freddie Prinze, Sr., star of the popular NBC sitcom *Chico and the Man*, committed suicide on January 29, 1977. Distraught over his recent divorce from Freddie's mother and under the influence of drugs, Prinze, Sr., died from a self-inflicted gunshot wound. The groundbreaking actor/comedian was only twenty-two at the time and had a very promising future. His tragic death stunned millions of fans. Despite his short life, the popular stand-up comedian with the infectious grin and bubbly personality was the inspiration for a generation of comics; but his

Freddie's father, Freddie Prinze, Sr., was the star of Chico and the Man, *a popular sitcom in the 1970s.*

Freddie Sr. with actor Jimmie Walker at a nightclub

story was also a cautionary tale about the dangers of celebrity and the temptation to use drugs.

Freddie Prinze, Jr., is determined to stay away from drugs. He declares he is "high every day" doing the thing he loves most— acting. "My dad taught me one of the most valuable lessons in the world through his death...because he accidentally killed himself while using drugs," Freddie told *People Weekly*. "That's why I'll never use them." Instead, he prefers to live a more low-key lifestyle, avoiding Hollywood parties. Freddie finds he has more fun spending time with friends, cooking, and playing video games, basketball, paintball, and miniature golf. He also has a great love for the martial arts and has trained in many different disciplines.

Freddie's mother, Katherine Cochran, now a real estate agent in Las Vegas, Nevada, was married to Freddie's father for two years. She blames the entertainment industry and its unbearable tensions, pressures, and easy access to drugs for her ex-husband's death. According to *The Los Angeles Times*, in 1981, Cochran and her former mother-in-law, Mary Preutzel, fought the coroner's ruling of "death by suicide" in court by suing the doctors who allegedly overprescribed drugs to Prinze and allowed him access to a pistol. They won over $1 million in out-of-court settlements.

Freddie has a great love for the martial arts and has trained in many different disciplines.

Traumatized by the incessant press coverage of her ex-husband's death, Katherine moved her four-year-old son from Los Angeles to Albuquerque, where her parents lived. She was determined to give Freddie the opportunity for a normal life instead of one plagued by the scandal of his father's death. In 1995, Freddie told *The Los Angeles Times*, "My mom knew it would have been rough for me to grow up in L.A., hearing all kinds of things about my dad. So she made the smart choice and raised me in the middle of the desert where nothing could happen.

Katherine was determined to give Freddie the opportunity for a normal life.

. . . I went to school, I went to church, and I had a nice, quiet, normal childhood."

Freddie was raised in the middle-class Northeast Heights section of the city, shadowed by the Sandia Mountains. Freddie's maternal grandparents played a large part in raising him for the first few years of his life. He had a very close relationship with his grandmother, and he says his grandfather taught him how to stand up for himself. During the summers, he went to Puerto Rico and spent time with his paternal grandmother.

Another significant role model in his life was Don Sandoval, the father of his best friend, Chris. Sandoval, a successful business owner, became a surrogate father to him, offering him advice whenever it was needed. "When we first met Freddie, he was in desperate need of a father type," he recently stated in *The Los Angeles Times*. "Even though Kathy was very loving, he was still looking for a man. I feel

Freddie's maternal grand-parents played a large part in raising him for the first few years of his life.

fortunate enough to have been able to be here for him."

Nevertheless, Freddie still missed having a father of his own. "It was very frustrating," he confided to *People Weekly*. "It hurt a lot growing up . . . sometimes I became angry because almost everybody I knew had an old man except me. That wears on you after awhile. It becomes like a rock that you have to push up a hill, which eventually rolls you over."

When he was twelve years old, his uncle Ron, who had been his father's manager, told Freddie the good stuff and the bad stuff about his father so that he could begin to learn how to cope with it. Freddie contends it was rough being a fatherless teenager and trying to deal with his emotions. His way of escaping was to either be alone or to take refuge in his comic books. "The story of my father upset me until I was twenty-one," he said to *The Boston Herald*. "Now, because we're doing the same thing, I can understand to a point

Freddie contends it was rough being a fatherless teenager and trying to deal with his emotions.

what my father was going through and I am able to express myself artistically."

Freddie is grateful that his mother has always been there to pick him up whenever he was down or feeling scared. "She never quit on me," he says. Much of what he learned about his father he learned like everyone else—by watching tapes of his shows and listening to his 1975 comedy album, *Looking Good.* But his mother also conveyed to him how much joy he brought to his father's life, and how his father's face would light up whenever he held him in his arms. His father used to call Freddie "Pie," a nickname he still carries.

At La Cueva High School, Freddie frequently cut classes and rarely studied. He hated high school and felt rejected by most of his classmates when he was there. According to his twelfth-grade literature teacher, Patsy Boeglin, the only time he showed any enthusiasm was when he read aloud in her class from the play *Oedipus Rex*.

At La Cueva High School, Freddie frequently cut classes and rarely studied.

Boeglin says Freddie was very quiet and sensitive. She also remembers that the young girls always found him cute and attractive, but she didn't think he was aware of it. The only classes that ever seemed to excite him were English and Drama.

Don Sandoval comments that Freddie exhibited the potential and talent to become an actor even in grade school. He was a member of the Albuquerque Children's Theater and the Duo Drama Company. Despite his mother's attempt to push him in other directions, Freddie was still drawn to acting.

"Acting is the only thing I'm good at," he said during an interview with *The Calgary Sun* (November 6, 1997). "I wasn't a good student and I wasn't the best athlete." Realizing that it would be difficult for him to get into college, Freddie figured he had nothing to lose. He decided to take a risk and try his luck in Hollywood.

Despite his mother's attempt to push him in other directions, Freddie was still drawn to acting.

Chapter 3
Back to Hollywood

After graduating from high school in 1994, Freddie took some local acting lessons, and then moved to Los Angeles later that year. He left Albuquerque with very little money and drove to Los Angeles in an old, beat-up pickup truck. He lived with a family friend in the San Fernando Valley and worked at his restaurant. He went to many auditions, but with little success. He recalls in *People Weekly* that it was very difficult in the beginning, and he often felt lonely and scared. "I spent a lot of nights crying. I had no one to talk to. But after six months I literally felt the hand of

Freddie went to many auditions, but with little success.

God on me. I dropped to my knees and cried. I felt love like I had never felt before. And things started to fall into place."

A friend introduced him to manager Ric Beddingfield of *Creative Artists Agency*. Beddingfield has remained his manager to this day. Eventually Freddie landed a four-line role in the TV show *Family Matters*, playing a tough kid who brings a gun to school. He was eighteen at the time and thrilled to get his "big break" on the hit sitcom. After hearing that he got the part, he immediately went to his father's grave in Forest Lawn and said, "Thank you. I hope to make you proud."

Thereafter, he appeared in some television movies and ABC After School Specials, including a starring role as a teen father in *Too Soon for Jeff*. He was also featured in *Detention: Siege at Johnson High*, co-starring Henry Winkler and Rick Schroeder, playing a hostage who becomes a hero.

Eventually Freddie landed a four-line role in the TV show *Family Matters*, playing a tough kid who brings a gun to school.

In 1996, Freddie auditioned for a small role in the movie *To Gillian on Her 37th Birthday* and got the part. The film was written by David Kelley (creator of the TV shows *Ally McBeal* and *The Practice*) and starred Kelley's wife, Michelle Pfeiffer, as well as Peter Gallagher, Kathy Baker, and Claire Danes. It was Freddie's big-screen debut. It also featured his first screen kiss. He received strong reviews for this film, in which he plays Claire Danes's cool and hip boyfriend who is covered in fake tattoos and piercings. However, he admitted to Jay Leno (who was a good friend of his father's) on *The Tonight Show* how nervous he was about kissing Danes: "I was too scared to even talk to her. I went into the bathroom and I locked the door. I got down on my hands and knees and prayed, 'Dear God, I'm not trying to be cool or smooth or anything. Just please don't let me throw up on this girl!'" Luckily, the kiss turned out to be as successful as his budding movie career.

In 1996, Freddie auditioned for a small role in the movie *To Gillian on Her 37th Birthday* and got the part.

Freddie with Genevieve Bujold in The House of Yes

He next starred in *The House of Yes* (1997), with Parker Posey, Josh Hamilton, Rachael Leigh Cook, Genevieve Bujold, and Tori Spelling. Both Bujold and Posey exclaimed that they found the actor "adorable." Working on the low-budget *House of Yes* is where Freddie finally began to understand what acting was all about. He cites Parker Posey's and director Mark Waters's passion and love for their craft as the reason why he fell in love with the acting profession.

Also in 1997, Freddie was featured in the enormously popular teen horror flick *I Know What You Did Last Summer*, co-starring Jennifer Love Hewitt, Sarah

Michelle Gellar, Ryan Phillippe, and Ann Heche. In the film, he stars as one of four recent high school graduates who initially try to cover up a drunken accident and possible murder. They are stalked by a mysterious psychopath. This movie and its sequel, *I Still Know What You Did Last Summer* (1998), with Jennifer Love Hewitt and Brandy, catapulted Freddie Prinze, Jr., to stardom and made him a huge teen idol.

In I Still Know What You Did Last Summer, *Freddie's character and his friends try to hide an accidental murder.*

In 1998, Freddie appeared in a television movie entitled *Vig*, which co-starred Peter Falk, Lauren Holly, and Timothy Hutton. He told *The Los Angeles Times* he feels blessed to have had the opportunity to work with veteran actor Peter Falk, who served as a mentor and inspiration for him. "He brought my work to a place where it literally shouldn't have been for another two or three years. That is how great he is," he says reverentially. "I was like a sponge and all I had to do was soak it up. It was probably the hardest character I ever did and he made it the easiest job I ever had. For that I owe him more than I'll ever be able to give."

Taking another break from slasher-film roles, Freddie exhibited his comedic abilities in his most successful movie to date, *She's All That* (1999). In the film he plays Zack, the senior class president, star jock, and the big man on campus, who takes a bet that he can transform Laney (Rachel Leigh Cook), a wallflower and outcast, into a prom

Peter Falk served as a mentor and inspiration for Freddie.

queen. "I was a dork in high school. I barely even got to go to the prom," he said in an interview with *Hollywood Online*. "If anything, I was more like Laney."

On *The Rosie O'Donnell Show*, Freddie told O'Donnell he was such a bad athlete in high school that he accidentally scored a soccer goal for the opposing team. They lost the game 1-0.

In She's All That, *Freddie bets that he can turn the class outcast into the prom queen.*

She's All That
*was one of
Freddie's most
successful movies.*

In *People* he recalled a beach scene in *She's All That* in which he had to show off his chest. The makeup person turned out to be a godsend: "This lady shaded me, and I looked up and Yo! I had a chest! They make it look like you have muscles! And it looked real!" Director Robert Iscove says that Freddie insisted on wearing a robe between takes and was very shy about drawing any attention to himself. "It's pretty refreshing," Iscove said.

This endearing film became a highly successful sleeper hit, showcasing Freddie's dimensions as an actor and legitimizing his superstar potential. With his intense gaze and winning smile, Freddie became a teen idol almost overnight. Rachel Leigh Cook, in an interview with the Associated Press, said, "Until you meet Freddie, you will not realize what a feat of acting this was for him. He's the nicest guy you will ever meet in your entire life."

She's All That showcased Freddie's dimensions as an actor and legitimized his superstar potential.

Chapter 4
Keeping it Real

Freddie still drives the same Dodge Ram pickup truck that he drove when he was eighteen.

As of the year 2000, Freddie makes more than $1 million per film, but he still drives the same Dodge Ram pickup truck he drove from Albuquerque to Los Angeles when he was eighteen. He is amazed by all the accolades and headlines he has received, and he sometimes finds it a little overwhelming. He told *The Record* in 1999 that he was truly rattled when he was mobbed outside the MTV headquarters in New York City's Times Square after an appearance. "It gets a little creepy, but I just try to do my thing and stay nice to everybody, and make sure they know that I do appreciate it. I don't want people to mistake fear for rudeness."

Success has kept him incredibly busy, but he has tried hard to "keep it real" and not get caught up in all the hype of being the new heartthrob. He remembers that it wasn't long ago when he was considered the high school nerd and no one wanted to be around him. Now, people walk up to him on the street and give him hugs and handshakes, and ask for his autograph. But, as he related to *The Los Angeles Times*, he is well aware that fame can

Freddie dated actress Kimberly McCullough for four years.

Freddie has never shied away from who he is or from the legacy of his father's name.

come with a price. "I did three movies in three months [*Down to You*, *Boys and Girls*, and *Head Over Heels*]. And it cost me a lot. It cost me my girlfriend [he had dated soap opera actress Kimberly McCullough for four years]. And it cost me time with my family. I'll never do that again."

Freddie Prinze, Jr., has never shied away from who he is or from the legacy of his father's name. He carries it with a great sense of pride. "I was blessed with it, and out of respect to my father, I wouldn't think of changing it to anything else," he told *USA Today*. Moreover, he is the first to admit that in many ways his father's name has been an advantage to him. He told *The Calgary Sun*, "My pop made a lot of people laugh and they're still grateful for that. And I'm grateful they were grateful, because it opened a lot of doors."

Chapter 5
Coming to Terms

Freddie admits it sometimes bothers him to be constantly asked questions and compared to his famous father, particularly when the majority of his young fans have never even heard of Freddie Prinze, Sr. It also has reawakened painful memories for his mother. He is very protective of her and has tried his best to shield her from the media frenzy as much as possible.

Although there are similarities in their rise to fame (both achieving it at an early age), his career has been very different from his father's. He still feels a certain amount of pressure whenever

Freddie admits it sometimes bothers him to be constantly compared to his famous father.

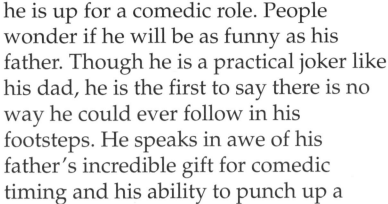

he is up for a comedic role. People wonder if he will be as funny as his father. Though he is a practical joker like his dad, he is the first to say there is no way he could ever follow in his footsteps. He speaks in awe of his father's incredible gift for comedic timing and his ability to punch up a joke. "The hardest job in the world is to make people laugh, and my father was brilliant," he said to *USA Today*. "I couldn't write a joke for anything."

Although Freddie can act, he says he doesn't have the same comedic ability his father had.

What Freddie Prinze, Jr., can do very well, however, is act. He has been able to do the one thing his father only dreamed about, and that is establish a successful movie career. That's why he finds it annoying when people try to label him as a "Latino" actor. When approaching a specific role, ethnicity is not as important to him as character. Freddie wants to do it all. He strives for great roles, and it doesn't matter whether his character is Spanish, Mexican, German, Irish, or whatever. His background reflects a rich cultural heritage. His father was half Puerto Rican and half Hungarian. His mother is English, Irish, and Native American. Freddie jokingly refers to himself as an "American mutt."

Freddie tries not to dwell on the negative emphasis the press frequently places on his father's death. He'd prefer that people focus more on the nature of his father's life, which he finds much greater and far more important. "I just want people to recognize my father as an artist who was way ahead of his time. He was a genius, and his life just burnt out quicker than it should have."

At times he truly wishes he could have had the chance to have spent time

Freddie tries not to dwell on the negative emphasis the press frequently places on his father's death.

"Not having a father makes me want to be a great one," says Freddie.

with his father and shown him how much love he has for him. But he is comforted by the thought that one day he might be able to shower that love on a child of his own. He told *People Weekly*, "Not having a father makes me want to be a great one."

Freddie acknowledges that there are times when he feels his father's presence. And that wherever he is, he knows his father has been looking out for him and is very proud of him. "Every once in awhile it really feels like he's here with me . . . and that's a really nice feeling."

Filmography

Family Matters (guest appearance) (1994)
Too Soon for Jeff (1996)
To Gillian on Her 37th Birthday (1996)
Detention: The Siege at Johnson High (1997)
The House of Yes (1997)
I Know What You Did Last Summer (1997)
Vig (1998)
I Still Know What You Did Last Summer (1998)
Sparkler (1999)
She's All That (1999)
Wing Commander (1999)
Down to You (2000)
Head Over Heels (2000)
Boys and Girls (2000)
Saturday Night Live (TV guest-host appearance) (2000)

Chronology

- Born March 8, 1976, in Los Angeles, California. Father: Freddie Prinze, famous comedian and star of the television sitcom *Chico and the Man*; mother: Katherine Cochran, a real estate agent.
- 1977, Freddie Prinze, Sr., despondent over a recent divorce and under the influence of drugs, kills himself in the prime of his career at age twenty-two; his son is only ten months old.
- 1981, Freddie's mother and grandmother sue doctors who they claim gave Prinze, Sr., access to the pistol he used to shoot himself and overprescribed tranquilizers. They receive over $1 million in out-of-court settlements. Katherine moves Freddie, Jr. to Albuquerque.
- 1994, Freddie graduates from La Cueva High School. Moves to Los Angeles to pursue acting.
- 1996, lands his first film role in *To Gillian on Her 37th Birthday*.
- 1997, stars in *I Know What You Did Last Summer*.
- 1999, his first romantic leading role in *She's All That* is a major success and establishes him as a heartthrob.
- 2000, stars in three movies; hosts *Saturday Night Live*

Index